THE ART OF JOYFUL LIVING

Build Personal Management Skills, Start Thinking Positive,

Conquer Challenges and Transform Your Life.

PRADIP DAS

© **Copyright 2024 - All rights reserved.**

The content contained within this book may not be reproduced, duplicated, or transmitted without direct written permission from the author or the publisher. Under no circumstances will any blame or legal responsibility be held against the publisher, or author, for any damages, reparation, or monetary loss due to the information contained within this book. Either directly or indirectly.

Legal Notice:

This book is copyright protected. This book is only for personal use. You cannot amend, distribute, sell, use, quote or paraphrase any part, or the content within this book, without the consent of the author or publisher.

Disclaimer Notice:

Please note the information contained within this document is for educational and entertainment purposes only. All effort has been executed to present accurate, up to date, and reliable, complete information. No warranties of any kind are declared or implied. Readers acknowledge that the author is not engaging in the rendering of legal, financial, medical or professional advice. The content within this book has been derived from various sources. Please consult a licensed professional before attempting any techniques outlined in this book.

By reading this document, the reader agrees that under no circumstances is the author responsible for any losses, direct or indirect, which are incurred as a result of the use of information contained within this document, including, but not limited to, — errors, omissions, or inaccuracies.

Author Profile

Table of Contents

Table of Contents 4
Introduction 5
Understanding Joy 12
Mindset Shift for Joy 21
Joyful Habits and Practices..................................... 29
Overcoming Challenges 38
Joy in Personal Development................................. 50
Joyful Living at Work... 60
Nurturing Joyful Connections................................. 71
Joyful Mindfulness Practices 82
Celebrating Success and Achievements.................. 92
Sustaining Joy in the Long Run 98
Conclusion.. 109

Introduction

Lionel Messi, a maestro on the field, symbolizes the essence of joyful living. Despite facing numerous challenges throughout his career, Messi has continually demonstrated the passion for the sport, a relentless pursuit of excellence, and a deep sense of fulfillment in doing what he loves most—playing football.

From his humble beginnings in Rosario, Argentina, to his meteoric rise to becoming one of the greatest footballers of all time, Messi's journey is a testament to the power of perseverance, resilience, and self-belief in one's dreams.

Joyful living covers a state of being characterized by happiness, contentment, and fulfillment in various aspects of life. While it may seem elusive at times, Messi's story reminds us that it is indeed possible. It's not about living a perfect life free from challenges or hardships but rather about finding joy and meaning amidst the inevitable ups and downs.

Just as Messi finds joy in the beautiful game of football, each individual has the opportunity to discover their own sources of joy—whether through pursuing passions, nurturing relationships, or simply finding contentment in the present moment.

Joyful living is expressed by happiness, contentment, and fulfillment in various aspects of life. It involves experiencing a deep sense of joy, gratitude, and satisfaction in everyday moments, relationships, activities, and accomplishments. Joyful living is not merely about experiencing short-lived moments of happiness but developing an overall sense of well-being and positivity.

Key aspects of joyful living include:

Gratitude: Practicing gratitude involves appreciating the abundance and blessings in one's life, both big and small. Gratitude raises a positive outlook, enhances emotional resilience, and cultivates a deeper sense of fulfillment.

Mindfulness: Being mindful involves being fully present and engaged in the present moment, without judgment or distraction. Mindfulness practices, such as meditation or mindful breathing, help individuals to savor experiences, reduce stress, and enhance overall well-being.

Purpose: Having a sense of purpose gives meaning and direction to life. It involves aligning one's actions, goals, and values with a greater sense of meaning or contribution to society, which fosters a sense of fulfillment and satisfaction.

Connection: Meaningful connections with others are essential for joyful living. Building and nurturing relationships with friends, family, and community members provide support, companionship, and opportunities for shared experiences, laughter, and growth.

Self-care: Prioritizing self-care involves taking care of one's physical, emotional, and mental well-being. Engaging in activities that promote relaxation, health, and personal growth, such as exercise, hobbies, or spending time in nature, contribute to a sense of vitality and happiness.

Resilience: Developing resilience enables individuals to bounce back from adversity and challenges with strength and grace. Developing coping strategies, positive thinking patterns, and a growth mindset fosters resilience and enables individuals to navigate life's ups and downs with greater ease.

Overall, joyful living is about accept life with open arms, finding beauty and meaning in everyday experiences, nurturing relationships, and prioritizing self-care and personal growth. It involves developing a mindset of gratitude, mindfulness, and resilience that allows individuals to find joy and fulfillment amidst life's inevitable challenges and uncertainties.

Importance of Nurturing Joy

Nurturing joy is crucial for overall well-being and personal fulfillment. Here are some key reasons why it's important:

Joyful experiences and positive emotions have been linked to improved mental health outcomes, including reduced levels of stress, anxiety, and depression. Nurturing joy can help individuals build resilience in the face of adversity and cope more effectively with life's challenges.

Research suggests that experiencing joy and happiness can have tangible benefits for physical health. Positive emotions have been associated with lower levels of inflammation, improved cardiovascular health, and a strengthened immune system. By Nurturing joy, individuals may experience better overall health and greater longevity.

Joyful individuals tend to be more resilient in the face of setbacks and adversity. Nurturing joy can help build emotional resilience, enabling individuals to bounce back from difficult situations more quickly and effectively. This resilience allows people to maintain a sense of optimism and hope, even during challenging times.

Joyful individuals often have more fulfilling and positive relationships with others. Nurturing joy can improve interpersonal connections by fostering empathy, kindness, and generosity. Joyful interactions with others can strengthen social bonds and contribute to a sense of belonging and community.

Joyful states of mind are conducive to creativity and innovation. When individuals experience joy, they are more likely to think creatively, problem-solve effectively, and generate new ideas. Nurturing joy can enhance productivity and performance in various aspects of life, including work, hobbies, and personal projects.

Ultimately, nurturing joy leads to greater overall life satisfaction and fulfillment. By focusing on positive experiences and nurturing feelings of joy, individuals can create a sense of meaning and purpose in their lives. Nurturing joy allows people to savor the present moment, appreciate life's blessings, and find joy in everyday experiences.

Nurturing joy is essential for mental, physical, and emotional well-being. By prioritizing activities and practices that bring joy into their lives, individuals can experience numerous benefits, including improved mental health, increased resilience, stronger relationships, enhanced creativity, and greater life satisfaction.

Understanding Joy

Exploring the nature of joy is a profound journey into the essence of happiness and fulfillment. Joy is a deep-seated emotion that surpasses mere satisfaction. Understanding joy involves exploring into its complex nature and unraveling the factors that contribute to its presence in our lives.

Joy exist in the human emotions, encompassing feelings of contentment, gratitude, and inner peace. It emerges not just from external circumstances but from our internal state of being, rooted in a sense of connection, purpose, and fulfillment.

Joy often blossoms in moments of mindfulness and presence, when we fully immerse ourselves in the present moment without judgment or attachment. By Nurturing awareness of our thoughts, sensations, and surroundings, we open ourselves to the beauty and wonder of life, inviting joy to permeate our experiences.

Joy flourishes in the context of meaningful connections and relationships with others. Whether through acts of kindness, shared experiences, or heartfelt conversations, the bonds we form with loved ones and our broader community nourish our souls and infuse our lives with joy.

Finding meaning and purpose in our lives is essential for experiencing lasting joy. When we align our actions with our values and aspirations, we tap into a profound sense of fulfillment that transcends momentary pleasures, anchoring us in a deeper sense of purpose and joy.

Joy is not immune to life's challenges and setbacks, but rather, it often emerges in the midst of adversity. Developing resilience and embracing growth through life's ups and downs allows us to find joy in the process of overcoming obstacles and evolving into our best selves.

We unlock the door to a life infused with joy—a life where every moment becomes an opportunity for discovery, wonder, and profound fulfillment by Developing mindfulness, gratitude, connection, purpose, resilience, and simplicity.

Factors Influencing Joy

Several factors contribute to the experience of joy, influencing both its occurrence and intensity. Here are some key factors:

Positive Events: Joy often arises in response to positive events or experiences. These can include achievements, celebrations, acts of kindness, or moments of success. Positive events trigger the release of neurotransmitters like dopamine and serotonin in the brain, which are associated with feelings of happiness and pleasure.

Gratitude: Developing a sense of gratitude can enhance the experience of joy. When individuals focus on the things they appreciate in their lives, whether big or small, it can foster feelings of contentment and happiness. Gratitude shifts the focus from what is lacking to what is present, amplifying the experience of joy in everyday moments.

Social Connections: Human beings are social creatures, and interpersonal relationships play a significant role in experiencing joy. Spending time with loved ones, sharing experiences, and feeling connected to others can elicit feelings of joy and fulfillment. Social support and positive interactions with friends, family, and community members contribute to overall well-being and happiness.

Mindfulness and Presence: Being fully present in the moment, practicing mindfulness, and engaging in activities that promote flow states can enhance joy.

Mindfulness involves paying attention to the present moment without judgment, which allows individuals to fully experience and appreciate life's simple pleasures. Engaging in activities that align with one's interests and values can also evoke a sense of joy and fulfillment.

Self-Expression and Creativity: Engaging in creative pursuits, expressing oneself authentically, and pursuing hobbies can bring about feelings of joy. Whether through art, music, writing, or other forms of self-expression, tapping into creativity allows individuals to connect with their inner selves and experience a sense of fulfillment. Creativity provides an outlet for self-discovery, exploration, and personal growth, leading to moments of joy and satisfaction.

Physical Well-being: Physical health and well-being play a crucial role in influencing joy. Regular exercise, adequate sleep, and a balanced diet contribute to overall feelings of well-being, energy, and vitality. Physical activity releases endorphins, neurotransmitters that act as natural mood lifters, promoting feelings of happiness and joy. Taking care of one's body through healthy lifestyle habits can positively impact mood and emotional state.

Purpose and Meaning: Having a sense of purpose, meaning, and fulfillment in life can significantly influence joy. When individuals feel that their lives have meaning and that they are contributing to something greater than themselves, it can bring about deep feelings of satisfaction and joy. Pursuing goals aligned with one's values, passions, and aspirations can instill a sense of purpose and fulfillment, leading to greater overall happiness.

Resilience: The ability to bounce back from adversity and navigate life's challenges with resilience can contribute to the experience of joy. Resilient individuals are better equipped to find silver linings in difficult situations, cultivate optimism, and maintain a positive outlook despite setbacks. Building resilience through coping strategies, self-care practices, and support networks can enhance one's capacity to experience joy even in the face of adversity.

These factors interact in complex ways to shape the experience of joy in individuals' lives.

Differentiating Joy from Happiness

Joy and happiness are often used interchangeably, but they represent distinct emotional states with unique characteristics and sources. While both joy and happiness are positive experiences that contribute to overall well-being, they manifest differently and are influenced by diverse factors.

Happiness is often associated with transient feelings of pleasure and contentment derived from external circumstances or events. It can be experienced in moments of achievement, success, or gratification, such as receiving praise for a job well done, enjoying a delicious meal, or spending time with loved ones. Happiness tends to be more fleeting and dependent on external factors, making it susceptible to fluctuations based on changing circumstances. For example, winning a competition or receiving a promotion at work may lead to feelings of happiness, but these emotions may diminish over time as the initial excitement fades or new challenges arise.

On the other hand, joy is a deeper and more enduring emotion that arises from within and is less dependent on external circumstances. Unlike happiness, which is often associated with specific events or outcomes, joy is a state of inner contentment and fulfillment that transcends momentary experiences. It can be found in simple pleasures, acts of kindness, or moments of connection with others. For instance, witnessing a beautiful sunset, engaging in a meaningful conversation, or expressing gratitude for life's blessings can evoke feelings of joy that linger long after the experience has passed.

Moreover, joy is often characterized by a sense of peace, gratitude, and spiritual fulfillment, whereas happiness may be accompanied by excitement, pleasure, or satisfaction. While happiness is fleeting and dependent on external factors, joy is more resilient and can be cultivated through practices such as mindfulness, gratitude, and self-reflection. By nurturing a mindset of joy, individuals can find solace and contentment even in the face of adversity or challenges, leading to a deeper sense of fulfillment and meaning in life.

In essence, happiness is like a passing breeze, while joy is like a steady flame that illuminates the path of life. While both emotions contribute to overall well-being, joy offers a more deep and enduring source of fulfillment that enriches the human experience.

Mindset Shift for Joy

Serena Williams, renowned as one of the greatest tennis players of all time, has not only dominated the sport with her unparalleled skill but has also exemplified a remarkable mindset shift towards joy throughout her career.

Early in her journey, Serena faced numerous challenges and setbacks, from racial discrimination to injuries and personal struggles. Despite these obstacles, she maintained an unwavering determination and a relentless focus on her passion for tennis.

However, it was during a particularly challenging period in her career that Serena experienced a profound mindset shift towards embracing joy. After facing defeat in several high-stakes matches and grappling with self-doubt, Serena realized that her happiness and fulfillment were not solely dependent on winning trophies or accolades.

Instead, she began to prioritize joy in every aspect of her life, both on and off the court. Serena found joy in the process of improvement, in the companionship with her fellow players, and in the support of her family and fans. She acceptd each match with a sense of gratitude and a genuine love for the game, regardless of the outcome.

This shift in mindset not only revitalized Serena's passion for tennis but also propelled her to new heights of success. With a renewed sense of joy and purpose, she went on to achieve countless victories, including multiple Grand Slam titles and Olympic gold medals.

Off the court, Serena's mindset shift towards joy has also influenced her entrepreneurial endeavors and philanthropic initiatives. She has become an advocate for women's empowerment, using her platform to inspire others to pursue their dreams with resilience, determination, and above all, joy.

In Serena Williams' story, we see the transformative power of accepting joy as a mindset.

Embracing a positive mindset is not just about seeing the world through rose-colored glasses; it's a transformative approach to life that can lead to greater joy and fulfillment. By developing positivity in our thoughts and actions, we open ourselves up to a wealth of opportunities and experiences that enrich our lives.

Adopt Positivity to Change the Mindset

One way to adopt a positive mindset is by practicing gratitude. Taking a moment each day to reflect on the things we are grateful for can shift our perspective and remind us of the abundance in our lives. For example, acknowledging the beauty of nature, appreciating the kindness of others, or simply expressing gratitude for our health and well-being can foster feelings of joy and contentment.

Another aspect of embracing positivity is adopting an optimistic outlook. Rather than dwelling on setbacks or challenges, focusing on solutions and possibilities can help us navigate life's ups and downs with resilience and hope. For instance, instead of viewing failures as roadblocks, we can see them as opportunities for growth and learning, ultimately leading to greater personal development and satisfaction.

Surrounding ourselves with positivity can have a profound impact on our well-being. Spending time with supportive friends and family members, engaging in activities that bring us joy and fulfillment, and consuming uplifting content can all contribute to a more positive mindset. By consciously choosing to fill our lives with positivity, we create an environment that nurtures happiness and optimism.

Letting Go of Negativity

Letting go of negativity opens the door to joy and inner peace. It begins with a conscious decision to release the weight of negative emotions, thoughts, and beliefs that hold us back from experiencing true happiness. Imagine carrying a heavy backpack filled with resentment, anger, and self-doubt everywhere you go. It weighs you down, drains your energy, and clouds your perception of the world. But what if you could unzip that backpack and let go of its burdensome contents?

Letting go of negativity is not always easy. It requires courage, self-awareness, and a willingness to confront uncomfortable truths. However, the rewards are immeasurable. By releasing the grip of negativity, we create space for joy, gratitude, and abundance to flow into our lives. We become more present, more compassionate, and more resilient in the face of life's challenges. Ultimately, letting go of negativity is a powerful act of self-love and empowerment that paves the way for a life filled with joy, purpose, and fulfillment.

Practicing Gratitude

Gratitude is a powerful practice that can infuse our lives with joy and contentment. By developing an attitude of thankfulness for the blessings, big and small, that surround us, we open ourselves up to experiencing greater fulfillment and happiness. Take, for instance, the simple pleasure of savoring a warm cup of coffee on a chilly morning. By pausing to appreciate the aroma, the flavor, and the comfort it brings, we can transform an everyday moment into one of gratitude and joy.

Gratitude also has the remarkable ability to shift our perspective, helping us find silver linings even in challenging situations. Consider a setback at work or in personal life; instead of dwelling on the negative aspects, practicing gratitude allows us to focus on the lessons learned, the strength gained, or the support received from others. For example, facing a professional setback may prompt us to reflect on the skills we've developed, the relationships we've forged, or the opportunities for growth that lie ahead, fostering a sense of optimism and resilience.

Furthermore, expressing gratitude towards others strengthens our connections and deepens our relationships, enhancing our overall sense of joy and well-being. Whether it's a heartfelt thank-you note to a colleague, a kind gesture towards a friend, or a simple acknowledgment of someone's efforts, expressing gratitude fosters positive interactions and fosters a sense of belonging and appreciation. For instance, thanking a friend for their support during a difficult time not only strengthens the bond between you but also brings joy to both the giver and the receiver.

While nurturing an attitude of thankfulness, shifting our perspective towards the positive, and expressing gratitude towards others, we can experience greater happiness, fulfillment, and connection in our daily lives.

Joyful Habits and Practices

Daily rituals for joy are simple yet intentional practices that can enhance your overall well-being and bring a sense of happiness and fulfillment to your life. Following are some daily rituals you can incorporate into your routine to cultivate joy:

Gratitude Practice: Start your day by expressing gratitude for the blessings in your life. Take a few moments each morning to reflect on things you're thankful for, whether it's your health, loved ones, or opportunities. Keeping a gratitude journal can help you cultivate a positive mindset and appreciate the abundance in your life.

Mindful Moments: Incorporate mindfulness into your daily routine by taking moments to pause, breathe, and center yourself. Whether it's through meditation, mindful walking, or simply savoring a cup of tea, mindfulness can help you cultivate presence and find joy in the present moment.

Connection: Make time to connect with loved ones each day, whether it's through a phone call, video chat, or spending quality time together. Building and nurturing relationships is essential for fostering joy and a sense of belonging.

Movement: Prioritize movement and physical activity each day to boost your mood and energy levels. Whether it's going for a walk, practicing yoga, or dancing to your favorite music, find ways to move your body that bring you joy and vitality.

Creativity: Engage in creative activities that bring you joy and allow you to express yourself. Whether it's painting, writing, cooking, or gardening, find outlets for your creativity that bring a sense of fulfillment and inspiration.

Nature Connection: Spend time in nature each day, whether it's a walk in the park, gardening, or simply sitting outside and soaking in the beauty around you. Connecting with nature can have a calming and rejuvenating effect, enhancing your overall sense of well-being.

Acts of Kindness: Practice random acts of kindness each day, whether it's complimenting someone, offering assistance, or simply smiling at a stranger. Acts of kindness not only brighten someone else's day but also bring joy and fulfillment to your own life.

Reflection: Take time each evening to reflect on your day and acknowledge moments of joy, accomplishment, and growth. Developing a habit of reflection can help you appreciate the beauty and richness of life, even in the midst of challenges.

Unplug and Recharge: Set boundaries around technology and take regular breaks from screens to recharge and reconnect with yourself. Spend time engaging in activities that nourish your soul, such as reading, listening to music, or practicing self-care.

Gratitude Practice: End your day by expressing gratitude once again, reflecting on the positive moments and experiences you've had throughout the day. Developing a mindset of gratitude can help you shift your focus from what's lacking to what's abundant in your life, fostering a sense of joy and contentment.

By incorporating these daily rituals into your life, you can cultivate joy, gratitude, and fulfillment each day, leading to a happier and more meaningful existence.

Mindfulness and Presence

"Mindfulness and Presence in Joyful Practices and Habits" explores the deep impact of mindfulness on Developing joy and contentment in everyday life. Through a journey of self-discovery and reflection, readers uncover the transformative power of being fully present in each moment, embracing simple yet meaningful practices that nurture happiness and fulfillment.

In this enlightening exploration, readers learn to harness the power of mindfulness to infuse joy into their daily routines and habits. Through mindfulness practices such as meditation, deep breathing, and mindful movement, readers cultivate a sense of inner peace and tranquility that permeates every aspect of their lives.

By maintaining a non-judgmental attitude and embracing acceptance of the present moment, readers learn to navigate life's challenges with grace and compassion. They discover that true joy arises not from external circumstances but from within, rooted in a profound sense of presence and mindfulness.

Through inspiring stories, practical exercises, and guided meditations, this book empowers readers to embark on a journey of self-discovery and transformation. It invites them to cultivate mindfulness as a way of life, integrating joyful practices and habits into their daily routines to cultivate lasting happiness and fulfillment.

Cultivating Joyful Relationships

Cultivating joyful relationships involves nurturing connections with others in a way that fosters mutual happiness, fulfillment, and growth. Here are some key strategies to cultivate joyful relationships:

Effective Communication: Open, honest, and empathetic communication is the foundation of any healthy relationship. Listening actively, expressing feelings and needs clearly, and providing validation and support are essential for building trust and understanding.

Quality Time Together: Spend meaningful time with loved ones, engaging in activities that bring joy and create shared experiences.

Whether it's going for a walk, cooking together, or simply enjoying each other's company, prioritizing quality time strengthens bonds and fosters connection.

Practice Gratitude: Express appreciation for the people in your life and acknowledge the positive impact they have. Cultivating gratitude fosters a deeper sense of connection and enhances overall well-being for both you and your loved ones.

Show Empathy and Compassion: Understanding and validating the emotions of others, even during challenging times, strengthens emotional bonds and fosters empathy. Showing compassion and support creates a safe space for vulnerability and deepens connection.

Foster Trust: Trust is essential for the foundation of any healthy relationship. Be reliable, honest, and consistent in your actions to build and maintain trust with your loved ones. Trust creates a sense of security and allows relationships to thrive.

Celebrate Achievements: Celebrate the successes and milestones of your loved ones, no matter how big or small. Sharing in each other's joys and accomplishments strengthens bonds and reinforces a sense of mutual support and encouragement.

Practice Forgiveness: Accept that conflicts and misunderstandings are a natural part of any relationship, and be willing to forgive and move forward. Letting go of grudges and practicing forgiveness promotes healing and allows relationships to grow stronger.

Set Boundaries: Establish clear boundaries that respect your own needs and the needs of others. Communicate openly about your boundaries and honor them to ensure mutual respect and understanding within the relationship.

Support Personal Growth: Encourage and support the personal growth and development of your loved ones. Celebrate their achievements, provide encouragement during challenges, and offer assistance when needed to help them reach their full potential.

Prioritize Self-Care: Take care of your own physical, emotional, and mental well-being to show up fully in your relationships. Prioritizing self-care allows you to bring your best self to your interactions with others and fosters a healthier dynamic within your relationships.

By incorporating these strategies into your interactions with loved ones, you can cultivate joyful, fulfilling relationships that bring happiness, support, and meaning to your life.

Overcoming Challenges

Overcoming challenges is an integral part of personal and professional growth, requiring resilience, determination, and adaptability. Here's how individuals can navigate and overcome challenges effectively:

Positive Mindset: Developing a positive mindset is essential for overcoming challenges. Viewing obstacles as opportunities for growth and learning rather than insurmountable barriers can help individuals approach challenges with optimism and resilience.

Goal Setting: Setting clear, achievable goals provides direction and motivation when facing challenges. Breaking down larger goals into smaller, manageable tasks allows individuals to focus on making progress, even in the face of adversity.

Problem-Solving Skills: Developing strong problem-solving skills equips individuals with the ability to identify challenges, analyze them effectively, and generate innovative solutions. Embracing a proactive approach to problem-solving empowers individuals to overcome obstacles more efficiently.

Seeking Support: It's important to recognize when support is needed and to reach out to others for assistance. Whether seeking guidance from mentors, collaborating with colleagues, or leaning on friends and family for emotional support, surrounding oneself with a supportive network can provide valuable resources during challenging times.

Adaptability: Flexibility and adaptability are crucial for navigating unexpected challenges and changes. Being open to new ideas, perspectives, and approaches allows individuals to adjust their strategies and pivot when necessary, effectively overcoming obstacles and moving forward.

Resilience: Resilience is the ability to bounce back from setbacks and persevere in the face of adversity. Building resilience involves developing coping mechanisms, practicing self-care, and maintaining a sense of perspective during difficult times.

Continuous Learning: Embracing a mindset of continuous learning enables individuals to acquire new skills, knowledge, and perspectives that can help them overcome challenges more effectively. Seeking out opportunities for growth and development fosters adaptability and resilience.

Self-Reflection: Taking time for self-reflection allows individuals to gain insights into their strengths, weaknesses, and areas for improvement. Reflecting on past challenges and successes can provide valuable lessons and inform strategies for overcoming future obstacles.

Maintaining Balance: Balancing work, personal life, and well-being is essential for building resilience and effectively managing challenges. Prioritizing self-care, setting boundaries, and allocating time for relaxation and rejuvenation can help individuals maintain perspective and resilience during difficult times.

Celebrating Successes: Acknowledging and celebrating successes, no matter how small, reinforces a positive mindset and builds confidence for overcoming future challenges. Recognizing achievements and milestones along the journey provides motivation and momentum for continued growth and resilience.

Resilience in the Face of Adversity

Resilience in the face of adversity is the remarkable ability of individuals to pass through difficult circumstances, bounce back from setbacks, and emerge stronger than before. In a world filled with uncertainties and challenges, resilience serves as a beacon of hope, guiding individuals through the darkest of times. At its core, resilience is not merely about enduring hardships passively but rather about actively adapting and thriving in the face of adversity.

One key aspect of resilience is the capacity to maintain a positive mindset amidst adversity. Rather than succumbing to despair or negativity, resilient individuals cultivate a sense of optimism and hope that propels them forward. They view challenges as opportunities for growth and learning, recognizing that every setback is a stepping stone towards greater resilience and personal development. This positive outlook enables them to persevere through adversity with courage and determination, refusing to be defined by their circumstances.

Moreover, resilience is closely intertwined with emotional intelligence and self-awareness. Resilient individuals possess a deep understanding of their emotions and reactions to stress, allowing them to regulate their responses effectively. They acknowledge their feelings without being overwhelmed by them, practicing self-care and seeking support when needed. By fostering emotional resilience, individuals can navigate through adversity with grace and resilience, maintaining their mental and emotional well-being even in the face of significant challenges.

Resilience is not solely an individual trait but also a product of supportive relationships and a sense of community. Resilient individuals often draw strength from their connections with others, relying on their support networks for encouragement, guidance, and reassurance during difficult times. These relationships provide a source of comfort and solace, empowering individuals to face adversity with resilience and fortitude. Additionally, a sense of belonging and shared purpose within a community fosters resilience on a collective level, enabling individuals to weather storms together and emerge stronger as a cohesive unit.

In the journey of life, adversity may be inevitable, but resilience ensures that individuals can navigate through it with courage, resilience, and hope, transforming obstacles into opportunities for growth and empowerment.

Transforming Pain into Growth

In life, challenges are inevitable. Whether they arise from unexpected setbacks, personal struggles, or external circumstances beyond our control, challenges have the power to evoke feelings of pain, frustration, and despair. However, amidst the turmoil, there exists a transformative opportunity to turn pain into growth, to emerge from adversity stronger, wiser, and more resilient than before.

The journey of transforming pain into growth begins with embracing the discomfort and acknowledging the emotions that accompany adversity. Instead of suppressing or avoiding pain, we must confront it head-on, allowing ourselves to fully experience the range of emotions that arise. By doing so, we create space for healing and growth, paving the way for profound personal transformation.

Central to the process of overcoming challenges is reframing our perspective and finding meaning in adversity. Rather than viewing setbacks as insurmountable obstacles, we can choose to see them as opportunities for growth and learning. Adversity often serves as a catalyst for self-discovery, offering valuable insights into our strengths, weaknesses, and deepest desires. By reframing our mindset and embracing a growth-oriented outlook, we can extract lessons from adversity that propel us forward on our journey toward personal development.

The journey of transforming pain into growth requires resilience and perseverance in the face of adversity. It involves summoning the courage to confront our fears, push beyond our comfort zones, and accept discomfort as a necessary step toward growth. Resilience enables us to navigate the challenges of life with grace and determination, refusing to be defined by our circumstances and instead choosing to rise above them.

Ultimately, the process of transforming pain into growth is not linear but rather cyclical, marked by moments of progress and setbacks, triumphs and failures. It is a journey of self-discovery, self-awareness, and self-empowerment, guided by the belief that even in the darkest of times, there exists the potential for growth and renewal. As we accept the challenges that life presents us and commit to the journey of personal transformation, we unlock the inherent resilience and strength within ourselves, emerging from adversity not merely unscathed but transformed, empowered, and ready to accept the limitless possibilities that lie ahead.

Finding Joy in the Ordinary

It's easy to overlook the beauty and joy that exist in the ordinary moments. Yet, it is precisely in these seemingly mundane experiences that we often find the strength and resilience to overcome life's challenges. Finding joy in the ordinary is not about seeking grand gestures or extraordinary events; it's about embracing the simple pleasures that surround us each day.

One of the keys to finding joy in the ordinary is developing a mindset of gratitude. By appreciating the small blessings in our lives – a warm cup of tea in the morning, a shared laugh with a friend, or the beauty of a sunset – we can shift our focus away from the difficulties we face and towards the abundance that surrounds us. Gratitude allows us to see the silver linings in even the darkest of clouds, helping us to find joy and contentment amidst adversity.

Rather than constantly chasing after future goals or dwelling on past regrets, we learn to savour the simple pleasures of everyday life. Whether it's taking a leisurely stroll in nature, savouring a home-cooked meal, or spending quality time with loved ones, being present allows us to fully immerse ourselves in the richness of each moment. In doing so, we cultivate a sense of peace and contentment that can sustain us through life's ups and downs.

When we learn to appreciate the small moments of joy and beauty that exist all around us, we become better equipped to navigate the inevitable hardships that life throws our way. Rather than allowing difficulties to overwhelm us, we draw strength from the knowledge that joy can be found even in the darkest of times. This resilience enables us to face adversity with courage and grace, knowing that joy is always within reach, no matter what life may bring.

So, let us take a moment to pause, to breathe, and to appreciate the ordinary miracles that surround us each day – for therein lies the key to true happiness and fulfilment.

Joy in Personal Development

Personal development is often perceived as a journey of growth, a path towards self-improvement, and a quest for realizing one's full potential. Yet, amidst the pursuit of goals and the striving for success, the element of joy can sometimes be overlooked. However, joy is not merely a byproduct of personal development; it is an integral component that infuses vitality and meaning into the journey itself.

Personal development is about nurturing a deeper understanding of oneself, uncovering strengths, and addressing areas for growth. It involves setting goals, acquiring new skills, and developing habits that align with one's values and aspirations. While the pursuit of these objectives may entail challenges and obstacles, it is the sense of joy derived from progress and self-discovery that fuels the journey forward.

Joy in personal development manifests in various forms, from the exhilaration of achieving milestones to the satisfaction of overcoming setbacks. It is the thrill of learning something new, the gratification of honing skills, and the fulfillment of contributing to one's personal and professional growth. Moreover, joy arises from the sense of empowerment that comes from taking ownership of one's life and actively shaping its trajectory.

Joy in personal development is not solely derived from individual achievements but also from the connections forged along the way. It is the camaraderie of learning and growing together with like-minded individuals, the encouragement of mentors and peers, and the sense of community that fosters a supportive environment for growth. Sharing experiences, insights, and successes with others amplifies the joy of personal development, transforming it into a collaborative and enriching journey.

Finally, joy in personal development is not a fleeting emotion but a state of being—an inherent part of the journey towards self-actualization and fulfillment. It is the realization that growth is not just about reaching a destination but embracing the process with enthusiasm and gratitude. By infusing joy into every step of the journey, individuals can cultivate a sense of fulfillment, resilience, and zest for life that transcends the pursuit of goals alone.

Setting and Achieving Joyful Goals

Setting and achieving joyful goals is not just about reaching a destination; it's a transformative journey that infuses every step with purpose, fulfillment, and happiness. At its core, joyful goal-setting involves aligning our aspirations with our deepest desires and values, fostering a sense of meaning and satisfaction in our endeavors. By imbuing our goals with joy, we not only enhance our motivation and resilience but also cultivate a sense of contentment and well-being along the way.

The process of setting joyful goals begins with introspection and self-discovery. We must first clarify what brings us genuine happiness and fulfillment, understanding our passions, strengths, and values. This self-awareness forms the foundation upon which we can build goals that resonate with our authentic selves, ensuring that our pursuits are aligned with our deepest aspirations. Whether it's pursuing a career that aligns with our passions, nurturing meaningful relationships, or embarking on personal growth journeys, joyful goal-setting starts with honoring our true desires.

Once we've identified our aspirations, the next step is to translate them into clear, actionable goals. Setting joyful goals involves striking a balance between ambition and feasibility, ensuring that our objectives are both inspiring and attainable. By breaking down our larger aspirations into smaller, manageable tasks, we can create a roadmap for progress that celebrates each step forward. Moreover, infusing our goals with a sense of joy involves framing them in a positive light, focusing on the potential for growth, learning, and fulfillment rather than dwelling on challenges or setbacks.

Challenges and obstacles are inevitable along the way, but by embracing them as opportunities for growth and learning, we can navigate them with grace and perseverance. Maintaining a sense of optimism and gratitude allows us to stay grounded amidst adversity, reminding us of the joy inherent in the pursuit of our aspirations. Moreover, by staying connected to our sense of purpose and values, we can anchor ourselves during times of uncertainty, finding meaning and fulfillment in even the most challenging moments.

Ultimately, the true essence of setting and achieving joyful goals lies not just in reaching the destination but in savoring the journey itself. Each step forward, no matter how small, is an opportunity to experience joy, growth, and fulfillment.

Continuous Learning and Growth

Continuous learning and growth are essential components of personal and professional development, serving as catalysts for advancement and success in various aspects of life. In today's rapidly evolving world, the ability to adapt, acquire new skills, and expand one's knowledge base is more critical than ever. Continuous learning encompasses a mindset of curiosity, a commitment to improvement, and a willingness to accept change.

At its core, continuous learning is about recognizing that learning is not limited to formal education but is a lifelong journey of exploration and discovery. It involves seeking out opportunities for growth in every experience, whether through formal training programs, self-directed study, or experiential learning.

Continuous learning is not only beneficial for personal development but also essential for professional growth and success. In today's dynamic job market, employers value employees who demonstrate a commitment to learning and development. Moreover, in a rapidly evolving economy driven by innovation and technology, continuous learning is essential for staying ahead of the curve and remaining competitive in the workforce.

Continuous learning creates a culture of innovation and creativity within organizations, driving progress and success. When individuals are encouraged to explore new ideas, experiment with novel approaches, and challenge the status quo, it fuels a culture of innovation that propels organizations forward. By fostering a learning environment where employees feel empowered to share knowledge, collaborate on projects, and pursue new initiatives, organizations can harness the collective intelligence and creativity of their workforce to drive growth and achieve their goals.

Continuous learning and growth are fundamental pillars of personal and professional development, enabling individuals to adapt, thrive, and succeed in an ever-changing world. Whether through formal education, self-directed study, or experiential learning, the pursuit of continuous learning is a lifelong journey of discovery and growth that enriches lives, expands horizons, and unlocks new opportunities for success.

Self-Reflection for Joyful Living

Self-reflection is the mirror through which we perceive our inner world, providing a pathway to joyful living. Taking moments to pause and turn inward allows us to connect with our true selves, understand our emotions, and cultivate a sense of inner peace and fulfillment. Through self-reflection, we set up a journey of self-discovery, exploring the depths of our thoughts, feelings, and desires.

Self-reflection is a process of going to the beneath the surface of our consciousness to uncover the underlying beliefs, patterns, and motivations that shape our lives. By shining a light on our inner landscape, we gain clarity and insight into who we are and what brings us joy.

Self-reflection also serves as a powerful tool for personal growth and development. As we engage in introspective practices, we become more attuned to our strengths, weaknesses, and areas for improvement. We gain a deeper understanding of our values, passions, and aspirations, empowering us to align our actions with our authentic selves. Through self-reflection, we cultivate self-awareness, resilience, and a greater sense of purpose, paving the way for a more meaningful and fulfilling life.

Moreover, self-reflection fosters a sense of gratitude and appreciation for the present moment. As we reflect on the beauty and abundance that surrounds us, we tap into a wellspring of joy and contentment that transcends external circumstances. Through the practice of self-reflection, we learn to accept life with open arms, savoring each moment with a sense of wonder and awe.

Self-reflection is the gateway to joyful living, offering us a great opportunity to connect with ourselves on a deeper level and build a life of meaning and purpose. Through self-reflection, we uncover the wisdom, strength, and resilience that reside within us, guiding us towards a life of joy, authenticity, and abundance.

Joyful Living at Work

Finding joy and fulfillment can often seem like an elusive pursuit. However, developing a sense of joy and contentment at work is not only possible but also essential for overall well-being and productivity. Joyful living at work goes beyond mere satisfaction with tasks or achievements; it involves creating a positive mindset, fostering meaningful connections, and finding purpose in one's contributions.

Approaching each day with optimism, gratitude, and resilience can transform the way we perceive and engage with our work. Rather than viewing challenges as insurmountable obstacles, a positive mindset allows us to see them as opportunities for growth and learning. When we reframe setbacks as stepping stones to success, we can sail through the ups and downs of work life with greater ease and enthusiasm.

Building meaningful connections with colleagues and developing a sense of community within the workplace are also integral to joyful living at work. Human connections are fundamental to our well-being, and the relationships we cultivate at work can significantly impact our overall happiness and job satisfaction. Taking the time to connect with coworkers on a personal level, offering support and encouragement, and celebrating each other's successes can create a more positive and uplifting work environment.

Furthermore, finding purpose and meaning in our work is essential for experiencing joy and fulfillment. When we understand how our contributions align with our values and goals, work becomes more than just a series of tasks; it becomes a source of inspiration and motivation. Whether it's making a difference in the lives of others, contributing to a larger mission, or honing our skills and talents, finding purpose in our work can infuse each day with a sense of significance and satisfaction.

Joyful living at work is not about escaping from challenges or seeking constant happiness; it's about embracing a positive mindset, building meaningful connections, and finding purpose in our contributions. By adopting these elements in our work life, we can experience greater fulfillment, resilience, and overall well-being. Ultimately, joyful living at work is not only beneficial for individuals but also for teams and organizations, fostering a culture of positivity, collaboration, and success.

Creating a Positive Work Environment

Creating a positive work environment is essential for fostering joyful living at work, where employees feel valued, motivated, and fulfilled. Such an environment not only enhances individual well-being but also contributes to higher levels of productivity, creativity, and collaboration within the organization.

One key aspect of cultivating a positive work environment is fostering a culture of appreciation and recognition. When employees feel appreciated for their contributions and achievements, they are more likely to feel motivated and engaged in their work. This can be achieved through various means, such as regular recognition programs, verbal praise, or small gestures of appreciation. By acknowledging and celebrating the efforts of employees, organizations can create a sense of belonging and positivity that boosts morale and fosters joyful interactions among team members.

Another important factor in creating a positive work environment is promoting open communication and transparency. Employees prosper in an environment where they feel heard, respected, and informed about organizational decisions and changes. Encouraging open dialogue, soliciting feedback, and addressing concerns can help build trust and build a sense of psychological safety within the workplace. When employees feel comfortable expressing their ideas, concerns, and opinions, it promotes a culture of collaboration and mutual respect, leading to greater satisfaction and joy at work.

Providing opportunities for growth and development is essential for creating a positive work environment. Employees are more likely to feel fulfilled and motivated when they have opportunities to learn new skills, take on challenging projects, and advance in their careers. Investing in employee training and development programs, offering mentorship opportunities, and providing clear pathways for advancement can empower employees to reach their full potential and experience a sense of purpose and fulfillment in their work. When employees feel supported in their professional growth, it enhances their overall job satisfaction and contributes to a more positive and joyful work environment.

Lastly, promoting work-life balance and prioritizing employee well-being is crucial for creating a positive work environment conducive to joyful living. Recognizing that employees have lives outside of work and respecting their personal boundaries helps prevent burnout and promotes overall well-being. Offering flexible work arrangements, promoting wellness initiatives, and encouraging time off for rest and rejuvenation demonstrate a commitment to employee health and happiness. When employees feel supported in balancing their work and personal lives, it fosters a sense of gratitude, contentment, and joy that positively impacts their overall quality of life.

Creating a positive work environment is essential for fostering joyful living at work. Investing in employee well-being and happiness not only benefits individuals but also contributes to organizational success, productivity, and overall satisfaction. By prioritizing joy and positivity in the workplace, organizations can create a culture that inspires creativity, collaboration, and success.

Finding Purpose in Professional Life

Finding purpose in our work is essential for developing a sense of joy and fulfillment. Purpose serves as a guiding light, shaping our actions, decisions, and overall outlook on our professional lives. It transcends mere job descriptions and paycheck motivations, providing us with a deeper reason to engage in our work and contribute meaningfully to our organizations and communities.

One of the key elements of finding purpose in professional life is aligning our work with our values and passions. When we are able to pursue tasks and projects that resonate with what matters most to us, whether it's making a positive impact on society, fostering innovation, or promoting sustainability, our work becomes more meaningful and fulfilling. This alignment allows us to tap into our intrinsic motivations, driving us to excel and derive satisfaction from our contributions.

Finding purpose in our professional endeavors involves recognizing the broader impact of our work. Whether we're in customer service, finance, healthcare, or any other field, every role plays a part in serving a larger purpose or mission. By understanding how our individual efforts contribute to the collective goals of our organization or industry, we can find greater meaning in the tasks we perform daily. This perspective shift allows us to see beyond the immediate challenges or frustrations and appreciate the significance of our contributions to the greater good.

As our values, interests, and circumstances evolve, so too may our sense of purpose in our work. It's essential to regularly assess and reassess what drives us, what brings us joy, and what we hope to achieve through our professional endeavors. This self-awareness enables us to make intentional choices about our career paths, seek out opportunities that align with our evolving sense of purpose, and cultivate a sense of fulfillment in our work.

Balancing Work and Joy

Achieving a balance between work and joy is essential for fostering a fulfilling and joyful life, particularly in the context of the workplace. While work is a significant aspect of our lives and often necessary for financial stability and personal growth, neglecting joy and happiness can lead to burnout, stress, and dissatisfaction. Therefore, integrating joy into the work environment is paramount for promoting overall well-being and productivity.

First and foremost, finding joy in work involves developing a positive mindset and embracing a sense of purpose. When individuals derive meaning and fulfillment from their work, it becomes more than just a means to an end; it becomes a source of joy and satisfaction. This can be achieved by aligning personal values with professional goals, pursuing work that resonates with one's passions and interests, and focusing on the positive aspects of the job.

Promoting a culture of appreciation and gratitude within the workplace can significantly enhance joy and overall morale. Recognizing and acknowledging the efforts and achievements of colleagues, expressing gratitude for teamwork and collaboration, and celebrating milestones and successes can create a positive and uplifting atmosphere. Acts of kindness, encouragement, and support not only foster stronger relationships among coworkers but also contribute to a sense of belonging and camaraderie, further enhancing the joy experienced in the workplace.

Additionally, promoting work-life balance and prioritizing well-being is crucial for sustaining joy in the workplace. Encouraging employees to take breaks, pursue hobbies and interests outside of work, and prioritize self-care fosters a healthier and more balanced approach to work. Flexible work arrangements, such as remote work options or flexible hours, can also empower individuals to better manage their time and responsibilities, reducing stress and allowing for greater opportunities for joy and fulfillment both inside and outside the workplace.

Therefore, balancing work and joy is essential for developing a fulfilling and joyful life, particularly in the context of the workplace. Ultimately, integrating joy into the workplace not only enhances individual happiness and satisfaction but also leads to greater productivity, creativity, and overall success.

Nurturing Joyful Connections

Nurturing joyful connections enriches our lives and deepens our sense of belonging and fulfillment. At its core, fostering these connections involves developing meaningful relationships with others, rooted in empathy, compassion, and authenticity. These connections serve as the foundation of our social support networks, offering comfort, understanding, and shared experiences that bring joy and enrichment to our lives.

One of the key elements in nurturing joyful connections is the practice of active listening and empathetic communication. By truly listening to others with an open heart and mind, we create space for deeper understanding and connection. Empathetic communication involves not only hearing what others are saying but also understanding their emotions and perspectives. This allows us to build trust and rapport, fostering genuine connections that transcend superficial interactions.

Another essential aspect of nurturing joyful connections is the cultivation of gratitude and appreciation for the people in our lives. Expressing gratitude for the presence and contributions of others strengthens our bonds and fosters a sense of mutual respect and admiration. Whether through heartfelt words of thanks, acts of kindness, or simply being present and supportive, expressing gratitude cultivates an atmosphere of positivity and warmth in our relationships.

Additionally, nurturing joyful connections involves embracing vulnerability and authenticity in our interactions with others. When we allow ourselves to be vulnerable and share our true selves with others, we create opportunities for deeper connection and intimacy. Authenticity invites others to do the same, fostering an atmosphere of trust and acceptance where meaningful connections can flourish. By embracing vulnerability and authenticity, we create space for genuine connections that bring joy, meaning, and fulfillment to our lives.

As we continue to nurture these connections, we not only enhance our own well-being but also contribute to the greater sense of community and interconnectedness in the world around us.

Building Meaningful Relationships

Building meaningful relationships is a foundation of nurturing joyful connections and enriching our lives with happiness and fulfillment. At the heart of these relationships lies genuine care, empathy, and understanding, which form the foundation of deep and lasting connections with others.

One of the key aspects of nurturing meaningful relationships is active listening. Truly listening to others, with empathy and without judgment, allows us to understand their perspectives, feelings, and needs. When we feel heard and understood, we are more likely to open up and share our thoughts and feelings authentically, deepening the connection further.

Another essential element of building meaningful relationships is reciprocity. Healthy relationships thrive on mutual give-and-take, where both parties contribute to each other's well-being and growth. This reciprocity can take many forms, from offering support and encouragement during challenging times to celebrating successes and achievements together.

Additionally, vulnerability plays a crucial role in fostering meaningful connections. When we allow ourselves to be vulnerable with others, we create opportunities for intimacy and emotional depth. Sharing our fears, insecurities, and hopes with trusted individuals builds intimacy and trust, strengthening the bond between us. It's through vulnerability that we can truly connect with others on a profound level, knowing that we are accepted and loved for who we are, flaws and all.

Moreover, developing empathy and compassion towards others is essential for nurturing joyful connections. Empathy allows us to understand and share the feelings of others, while compassion drives us to act with kindness and support. When we approach relationships with empathy and compassion, we create a safe and nurturing environment where everyone feels valued, respected, and cared for. By practicing empathy and compassion in our interactions with others, we foster a sense of belonging and connection that brings joy and fulfillment to both ourselves and those around us.

Building meaningful relationships is essential for nurturing joyful connections and enriching our lives with happiness and fulfillment. When we prioritize building meaningful relationships, we create a community of love, support, and understanding that uplifts and sustains us through life's challenges and triumphs.

Social and Community Engagement

Social and community engagement plays a pivotal role in fostering joyful connections and enhancing overall well-being. One of the key benefits of social and community engagement is the opportunity to connect with others on a deeper level. Whether through shared interests, common goals, or mutual experiences, engaging with like-minded individuals fosters a sense of camaraderie and belonging. Whether it's joining a local club, volunteering for a cause, or attending community events, these interactions provide avenues for forming new friendships and strengthening existing ones. Such connections bring joy and fulfillment as individuals share laughter, support, and memorable moments together.

Furthermore, social and community engagement offers a platform for personal growth and development. Engaging in community projects or volunteering opportunities also allows individuals to contribute their time and talents towards making a positive impact, fostering a sense of purpose and fulfillment. Through these experiences, individuals not only enrich their own lives but also contribute to the well-being of their communities, creating a ripple effect of joy and positivity.

Moreover, social and community engagement serves as a buffer against loneliness and isolation, which are known to have detrimental effects on mental and emotional health. By actively participating in social activities and forming meaningful connections, individuals can combat feelings of loneliness and strengthen their support networks. Whether it's attending social gatherings, joining interest-based groups, or simply reaching out to neighbors, these interactions provide opportunities for social connection and belonging. As individuals feel more connected to their communities and supported by their social networks, they experience greater resilience and overall well-being.

Social and community engagement is a powerful catalyst for nurturing joyful connections and enhancing quality of life. As communities come together to support and uplift one another, the collective joy and resilience that result pave the way for a brighter, more vibrant future. Through social and community engagement, individuals not only find fulfillment in their own lives but also contribute to the creation of thriving, interconnected communities where joy and connection abound.

Joyful Parenting and Family Life

Joyful parenting and family life are deeply interconnected, forming the foundation for nurturing strong and joyful connections within the family unit. At the heart of joyful parenting is the cultivation of a positive and supportive environment where love, understanding, and empathy thrive. It involves embracing the joys and challenges of parenthood with an open heart and a willingness to learn and grow alongside your children.

Central to joyful parenting is the practice of mindfulness and presence. Being fully present in the moment allows parents to connect more deeply with their children, fostering meaningful interactions and building trust and emotional bonds. By setting aside distractions and focusing on the here and now, parents can create moments of joy and connection that leave a lasting impact on their children's lives.

Furthermore, joyful parenting emphasizes the importance of nurturing a sense of playfulness and creativity within the family dynamic. Engaging in playful activities together not only brings laughter and joy into the home but also strengthens the parent-child relationship. Whether it's through imaginative play, outdoor adventures, or simple moments of silliness, embracing playfulness cultivates a sense of closeness and fosters a spirit of joy and spontaneity within the family.

In addition, joyful parenting extends to creating a harmonious and supportive family environment. This involves nurturing open communication, mutual respect, and a sense of belonging among family members. By fostering an atmosphere of trust and understanding, parents empower their children to express themselves authentically, share their thoughts and feelings, and cultivate healthy relationships within the family unit.

Overall, joyful parenting and family life are rooted in the principles of love, presence, and connection. Through intentional and heartfelt interactions, parents can embark on a journey of joyful parenting, creating cherished memories and nurturing lifelong relationships filled with love, laughter, and happiness.

Joyful Mindfulness Practices

Joyful mindfulness practices invite us to engage fully in the present moment, allowing us to savor the richness of life and discover joy in even the simplest of experiences. In a world filled with distractions and constant busyness, mindfulness offers us to slow down, tune into our senses, and appreciate the beauty of the present moment. Whether it's savoring the taste of a delicious meal, feeling the warmth of the sun on our skin, or listening to the soothing sounds of nature, mindfulness encourages us to immerse ourselves fully in the here and now. By developing this awareness, we can break free from the grip of worries about the future or regrets about the past, allowing us to experience a deep sense of joy and gratitude for the abundance of life.

One powerful mindfulness practice that can bring immense joy is the practice of gratitude. Taking time each day to reflect on the things we are grateful for—whether it's our loved ones, our health, or the simple pleasures of life—can shift our perspective and fill our hearts with joy. Gratitude reminds us of the countless blessings that surround us each day, helping us to cultivate a sense of abundance and appreciation for the richness of life's experiences. By developing gratitude, we can cultivate a deep sense of joy and contentment that permeates every aspect of our lives.

Another joyful mindfulness practice is the practice of loving-kindness meditation. This practice involves sending wishes of love, compassion, and well-being to ourselves and others. Joyful meditation helps us to promote empathy, reduce feelings of isolation, and foster deeper connections with others, ultimately leading to greater happiness and well-being.

In short, joyful mindfulness practices offer a gateway to experiencing the richness and beauty of life totally. As we continue on our journey of mindfulness, may we accept each moment with open hearts and minds, finding joy in the simple act of being alive.

Meditation and Mindful Breathing

Meditation and mindful breathing are integral components of joyful mindfulness practices, offering great benefits for both mental and physical well-being. Finding moments of peace and tranquility can be challenging, but through meditation and mindful breathing, individuals can cultivate a sense of calm and presence amidst the chaos.

Mindful breathing involves paying attention to the breath in a non-judgmental and present-focused manner. Mindful breathing not only calms the mind but also regulates the body's stress response, promoting relaxation and a sense of balance. Through regular practice, individuals can harness the power of mindful breathing to reduce stress, enhance concentration, and foster a greater sense of inner harmony.

Incorporating meditation and mindful breathing into daily life can have transformative effects on overall well-being. Whether practiced individually or as part of a group setting, these mindfulness techniques offer valuable tools for managing stress, enhancing emotional resilience, and developing a positive outlook on life. Moreover, the benefits of meditation and mindful breathing extend beyond the individual, influencing relationships, work performance, and overall quality of life. As individuals commit to regular practice and accept the journey of self-discovery, they unlock the potential for profound personal growth and fulfillment.

Finally, meditation and mindful breathing are powerful vehicles for developing joy and mindfulness in everyday life. Through these practices, individuals can tap into a deep wellspring of inner peace, happiness, and contentment, regardless of external circumstances.

Joyful Visualization Techniques

Joyful visualization techniques are powerful tools within the realm of joyful mindfulness practices, offering a pathway to cultivate positivity, creativity, and inner peace. Through the practice of joyful visualization, individuals harness the innate power of their imagination to create vivid mental images of their desires, dreams, and aspirations. By engaging in this practice regularly, individuals can unlock a myriad of benefits that contribute to their overall well-being and happiness.

One of the primary benefits of joyful visualization techniques is their ability to instill a sense of optimism and hope. When individuals visualize themselves achieving their goals or experiencing moments of joy and fulfillment, they tap into a reservoir of positive energy that fuels their motivation and determination. By immersing themselves in these uplifting mental images, individuals can overcome feelings of doubt and uncertainty, replacing them with confidence and belief in their ability to manifest their desires.

Moreover, joyful visualization serves as a catalyst for creativity and innovation. As individuals visualize themselves engaging in activities they enjoy or pursuing their passions, they stimulate their imagination and unlock new ideas and insights. This creative energy can be channeled into various aspects of life, from problem-solving and decision-making to artistic expression and personal growth.

Joyful visualization techniques are also instrumental in promoting inner peace and emotional well-being.

Joyful visualization techniques are invaluable tools for developing positivity, creativity, and inner peace within the practice of joyful mindfulness. With the power of their imagination, individuals can tap into a limitless reservoir of optimism, creativity, and emotional well-being. Through regular practice and dedication, joyful visualization becomes not only a technique but a way of life—a journey of self-discovery and transformation that leads to greater happiness, fulfillment, and harmony in all aspects of life.

Incorporating Mindfulness into Daily Life

Incorporating mindfulness into daily life can significantly enhance overall well-being and cultivate a sense of joy and contentment. Mindfulness, often defined as the practice of being fully present and engaged in the moment without judgment, offers numerous benefits when integrated into daily routines.

One way to incorporate mindfulness into daily life is through the practice of mindful breathing. Taking a few moments each day to focus on the breath can help anchor attention to the present moment and calm the mind. Mindful breathing can be practiced anywhere, whether during a morning routine, while commuting, or before bedtime, making it accessible and adaptable to various lifestyles.

Another joyful mindfulness practice is mindful eating. In today's fast-paced world, mealtimes are often rushed and distracted, leading to mindless consumption and disconnection from the sensory experience of eating. By slowing down and savoring each bite, individuals can deepen their appreciation for food and nourish both body and mind. Mindful eating involves paying attention to the colors, textures, and flavors of food, as well as the sensations of chewing and swallowing. By bringing awareness to the act of eating, individuals can foster a healthier relationship with food and cultivate gratitude for the nourishment it provides.

In addition to mindful breathing and eating, incorporating mindfulness into daily activities such as walking, showering, or even washing dishes can amplify feelings of joy and presence. Mindful walking, for example, involves tuning into the sensations of each step, feeling the ground beneath the feet, and noticing the sights and sounds of the surrounding environment.

Overall, integrating mindfulness into daily life through practices such as mindful breathing, eating, and engaging in routine activities with presence can enrich the quality of everyday experiences and promote a deeper sense of joy and fulfillment. Individuals can tap into a wellspring of inner peace and resilience, navigating life's ups and downs with greater ease and grace. Whether through formal meditation practices or informal moments of mindfulness throughout the day, embracing mindfulness can lead to a more joyful and meaningful existence.

Celebrating Success and Achievements

Celebrating success and achievements is an essential aspect of acknowledging and appreciating the milestones we reach in our personal and professional lives. It serves as a powerful tool for motivation, morale boosting, and fostering a positive culture of recognition. When we take the time to celebrate our accomplishments, no matter how big or small, we reinforce the value of hard work, dedication, and perseverance.

Firstly, celebrating success cultivates a sense of pride and accomplishment within individuals. Whether it's completing a challenging project, reaching a sales target, or achieving a personal goal, recognizing these achievements instills a sense of validation and satisfaction. It reaffirms our capabilities and fuels our confidence to take on new challenges and strive for even greater heights in the future.

Moreover, celebrating success strengthens team cohesion and camaraderie in professional settings. When teams come together to commemorate shared victories, it fosters a sense of unity and collaboration. Recognizing the collective efforts that contributed to the achievement reinforces the importance of teamwork and reinforces the bonds between team members. This, in turn, promotes a supportive and positive work environment where individuals feel valued and motivated to contribute their best.

Beyond the immediate impact on individuals and teams, celebrating success also has broader organizational benefits. It helps to reinforce organizational values and goals by highlighting the alignment between individual achievements and the overarching objectives of the organization. By publicly acknowledging and rewarding outstanding performance, organizations can inspire others to emulate similar behaviors and drive overall performance improvement.

In addition to its motivational and organizational benefits, celebrating success also contributes to employee engagement and retention. When employees feel recognized and appreciated for their contributions, they are more likely to feel a sense of loyalty and commitment to their organization. This, in turn, leads to higher levels of job satisfaction, lower turnover rates, and ultimately, a more stable and productive workforce.

Celebrating success and achievements is not just about acknowledging individual accomplishments; it's about fostering a culture of recognition, appreciation, and positivity. Whether in personal or professional settings, taking the time to celebrate milestones serves as a powerful motivator, strengthens team dynamics, reinforces organizational values, and enhances overall engagement and satisfaction. By prioritizing celebrations and making them an integral part of our lives and workplaces, we can inspire greatness, drive performance, and create a culture where success is not just celebrated but also cultivated and sustained.

The Role of Gratitude in Celebrations

Gratitude serves as a powerful catalyst in the celebrations of success and achievements, infusing these moments with deeper meaning, connection, and fulfillment. At its core, gratitude is the heartfelt acknowledgment of the goodness in our lives, including the accomplishments we've achieved and the support we've received along the way. When we take the time to express gratitude during moments of success, we not only honor our own efforts but also recognize the contributions of others who have played a role in our achievements.

One of the key roles of gratitude in celebrations is its ability to foster a sense of connection and unity among individuals. By expressing gratitude towards those who have supported us, whether it be friends, family, mentors, or colleagues, we acknowledge the interconnectedness of our journeys and the collective effort that has led to our success. This shared sense of appreciation strengthens relationships, builds bonds of trust, and cultivates a supportive community that celebrates each other's victories wholeheartedly.

Moreover, gratitude enhances the experience of success by amplifying feelings of joy, satisfaction, and fulfillment. When we pause to reflect on our accomplishments with gratitude, we shift our focus from what we lack to what we have achieved, instilling a sense of abundance and contentment. Rather than striving for the next goal without acknowledging our progress, gratitude invites us to savor the present moment, basking in the glow of our achievements with a deep sense of appreciation and satisfaction.

Moreover, practicing gratitude during celebrations of success cultivates a positive mindset and outlook on life. Gratitude acts as a natural remedy to feelings of entitlement, comparison, or inadequacy that may arise amidst achievements. Instead of becoming complacent, gratitude encourages us to adopt a mindset of abundance and possibility, fueling our motivation to continue pursuing our goals with optimism and resilience.

Therefore, gratitude plays a pivotal role in elevating the experience of celebrations of success and achievements. As we nurture a habit of gratitude in both our triumphs and challenges, we not only enrich our own lives but also contribute to a culture of appreciation, support, and joy that uplifts and inspires those around us.

Sustaining Joy in the Long Run

Sustaining joy in the long run requires a multifaceted approach that encompasses both internal and external factors, as well as a commitment to develop a positive mindset and lifestyle habits. At its core, sustaining joy is about practicing a deep sense of contentment and fulfillment that transcends momentary pleasures and endures through life's inevitable ups and downs.

One key aspect of sustaining joy is nurturing a resilient mindset that enables individuals to bounce back from adversity and maintain a sense of optimism in the face of challenges. Resilience allows us to navigate the inevitable setbacks and disappointments that life throws our way without losing sight of the larger picture. By reframing setbacks as opportunities for growth and learning, we can build a mindset that is resilient in the face of adversity, allowing us to sustain joy even during difficult times.

Besides, sustaining joy involves developing meaningful connections and relationships with others. Research consistently shows that social support and meaningful relationships are essential for overall well-being and happiness. Investing time and energy into nurturing relationships with family, friends, and community members can provide a source of emotional support, belonging, and fulfillment that sustains joy in the long run.

In addition to developing a resilient mindset and nurturing meaningful relationships, sustaining joy also requires attention to physical and emotional self-care. Engaging in regular exercise, prioritizing healthy eating habits, getting enough sleep, and managing stress are all important aspects of self-care that contribute to overall well-being and happiness. Similarly, practicing mindfulness and relaxation techniques can help individuals manage stress and cultivate a greater sense of inner peace and contentment. Ultimately, sustaining joy is about accepting life with open arms, finding meaning and purpose in everyday experiences, and developing a sense of gratitude and appreciation for the blessings that surround us.

Preventing Burnout

Preventing burnout and sustaining joy in the long run is a vital aspect of maintaining overall well-being and productivity. In today's fast-paced world, individuals often find themselves overwhelmed by the demands of work, personal responsibilities, and societal expectations. As a result, they may experience burnout, characterized by emotional exhaustion, cynicism, and reduced efficacy in both professional and personal domains.

One effective strategy for preventing burnout is to prioritize self-care and establish healthy boundaries. This involves recognizing one's limitations and learning to say no to excessive demands or commitments that can lead to overextension. By setting realistic expectations and allocating time for rest, relaxation, and activities that bring joy and fulfillment, individuals can safeguard their mental and emotional health.

Another crucial aspect of preventing burnout is developing resilience and practicing mindfulness. Resilience refers to the ability to bounce back from adversity and maintain a sense of balance and well-being amidst challenges. Mindfulness involves being fully present and aware of one's thoughts, feelings, and sensations without judgment. So, by following mindfulness practices such as meditation, deep breathing exercises, or yoga into their daily routine, individuals can enhance their ability to manage stress, regulate emotions, and develop a positive mindset.

Additionally, nurturing supportive relationships and seeking social connections can help buffer against burnout and promote long-term well-being. Surrounding oneself with friends, family members, or colleagues who offer empathy, encouragement, and companionship can provide a sense of belonging and emotional support during difficult times. Engaging in meaningful conversations, sharing experiences, and participating in group activities or hobbies can foster a sense of connection and camaraderie, reducing feelings of isolation and loneliness.

Identifying personal values, goals, and aspirations can provide a sense of direction and motivation, helping individuals stay focused and engaged in their pursuits.

Preventing burnout and sustaining joy in the long run requires a proactive approach to self-care, resilience-building, social connection, and purposeful living.

Adjusting to Life Changes

Adjusting to life changes is a crucial aspect of sustaining joy and fulfillment over the long run. Life is dynamic, and transitions, whether anticipated or unexpected, are inevitable. How we navigate these changes can profoundly impact our overall well-being and sense of happiness.

One key to adjusting to life changes is embracing a mindset of flexibility and adaptability. Rather than resisting or fearing change, viewing it as an opportunity for growth and transformation can foster resilience and inner strength. By accepting that change is a natural part of life, we open ourselves up to new possibilities and experiences. This mindset shift allows us to approach life changes with curiosity and openness, rather than with anxiety or apprehension.

Another important aspect of adjusting to life changes is maintaining a sense of perspective and gratitude. When faced with challenges or transitions, it can be easy to dwell on the negative aspects or to feel overwhelmed by the uncertainty of the future. However, by practicing gratitude and focusing on the positive aspects of our lives, we can cultivate a sense of resilience and optimism. Recognizing the blessings and opportunities that each day brings can help us navigate life changes with grace and appreciation.

Building a strong support network can be invaluable in times of transition. Surrounding ourselves with friends, family, mentors, and other sources of support can provide encouragement, guidance, and reassurance during periods of change. Whether seeking advice, a listening ear, or practical assistance, having a supportive community can help us feel less alone and more capable of navigating life's ups and downs.

Ultimately, adjusting to life changes requires a willingness to accept uncertainty, cultivate gratitude, and lean on our support networks for guidance and encouragement. By adopting a mindset of flexibility, maintaining perspective, and seeking support when needed, we can navigate life's transitions with resilience and grace, sustaining joy and fulfillment in the long run.

Building Resilience for Lasting Joy

Adjusting to life changes is an inevitable part of the human experience, and how we navigate these transitions can significantly impact our ability to sustain joy in the long run. Life is inherently dynamic, presenting us with a countless challenges, opportunities, and unexpected twists and turns. Whether it's starting a new job, moving to a different city, experiencing a loss, or facing health issues, each change brings its unique set of emotions and adjustments.

One of the keys to sustaining joy amidst life changes is developing resilience—the ability to bounce back from adversity and adapt to new circumstances. Resilience enables us to accept change with a sense of optimism and resourcefulness, rather than succumbing to feelings of helplessness or despair. By developing resilience, we can view life's challenges as opportunities for growth and transformation, rather than insurmountable obstacles.

Another essential aspect of sustaining joy during life changes is practicing mindfulness and self-awareness. Mindfulness involves being fully present in the moment, without judgment, and developing an attitude of acceptance towards our thoughts, feelings, and experiences. By tuning into our inner world with compassion and curiosity, we can better understand how life changes affect us and respond with greater clarity and emotional balance. Self-awareness allows us to recognize our strengths, limitations, and core values, guiding us in making choices that align with our deepest aspirations and bring us lasting fulfillment.

In addition, maintaining a supportive network of relationships can play a significant role in sustaining joy during life changes. Connecting with family, friends, mentors, and community members provides us with emotional support, encouragement, and perspective during challenging times. These relationships offer a sense of belonging and connection that can buffer against feelings of isolation and loneliness, fostering resilience and well-being. Additionally, seeking professional support from therapists, counselors, or support groups can provide valuable guidance and coping strategies for navigating life changes effectively.

Sustaining joy in the long run amidst life changes requires a combination of resilience, mindfulness, self-awareness, and supportive relationships. By developing these qualities and practices, we can navigate the ups and downs of life with greater ease, grace, and inner peace. While life changes may present challenges and uncertainties, they also offer opportunities for growth, self-discovery, and the deepening of our capacity for joy. As we accept the journey of life with an open heart and a willingness to adapt, we can discover the resilience and joy that reside within us, regardless of the circumstances we may face.

Conclusion

Finally, we come to understand that joy is not merely a fleeting emotion but a deliberate choice, a state of being we can cultivate within ourselves and share with the world. As we've journeyed through the wisdom and insights presented within these pages, we've discovered that joy is not dependent on external circumstances but springs forth from the depths of our own hearts.

Finally, the art of joyful living is a practice—an ongoing journey rather than a final destination. It requires mindfulness, gratitude, resilience, and an unwavering commitment to embracing life's beauty amidst its complexities. Through the power of love, kindness, and self-discovery, we can paint our existence with vibrant hues of joy, illuminating even the darkest corners of our lives.

In the end, it is not the grand achievements or material possessions that define a life well-lived, but rather the simple moments of connection, laughter, and inner peace that truly nourish the soul.

May your journey be filled with boundless joy, and may you continue to uncover the artistry of joyful living with every step you take.

Join My Community

https://community.askpndas.com

Please have a look of the other books in the series, "The Art of Living".

www.ingramcontent.com/pod-product-compliance
Lightning Source LLC
Chambersburg PA
CBHW050317230526
45471CB00005B/2228